DINOSAUR
ADVENTURES

The Triassic Period

Ashley Lee

Explore other books at:
WWW.ENGAGEBOOKS.COM

VANCOUVER, B.C.

WWW.ENGAGEBOOKS.COM

The Triassic Period: Level 1
Lee, Ashley 1995
Text © 2021 Engage Books

Edited by: Alexis Roumanis and Lauren Dick

Text set in Arial Regular.
Chapter headings set in Arial Black.

FIRST EDITION / FIRST PRINTING

LIBRARY AND ARCHIVES CANADA CATALOGUING IN PUBLICATION

Title: The Triassic period / Ashley Lee.
Names: Lee, Ashley, 1995- author.
Description: Series statement: Dinosaur adventures

Identifiers: Canadiana (print) 20210310065 | Canadiana (ebook) 20210310103
ISBN 978-1-77476-486-2 (hardcover)
ISBN 978-1-77476-487-9 (softcover)
ISBN 978-1-77476-489-3 (pdf)
ISBN 978-1-77476-488-6 (epub)
ISBN 978-1-77476-498-5 (audio)

Subjects:
LCSH: Readers
LCSH: Readers—Dinosaurs.
LCSH: Readers—Paleontology—Triassic.

Classification: LCC PE1117 .D56 2022 | DDC J428.6—DC23

Contents

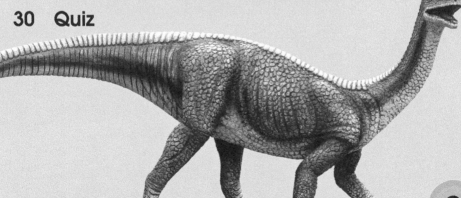

What Is the Triassic Period?

The Triassic Period is a time in Earth's history when dinosaurs first appeared.

It started about
252 million years
ago and ended about
201 million years ago.

What Were Triassic Dinosaurs?

Dinosaurs from the Triassic Period are called archosaurs (*aar-chow-sores*).

Archosaur means "ruling lizard."

What Did Triassic Dinosaurs Look Like?

Triassic dinosaurs came in all shapes and sizes. Some archosaurs walked on four legs and some walked on two legs.

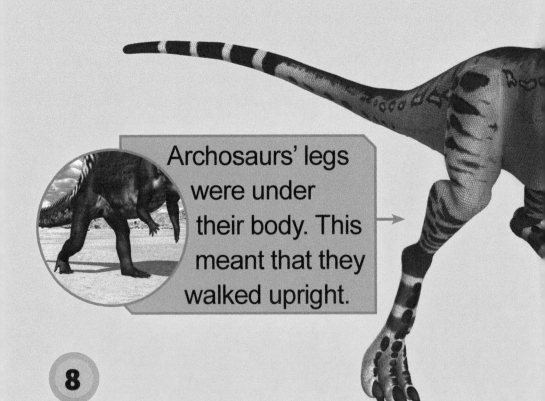

Archosaurs' legs were under their body. This meant that they walked upright.

Archosaurs had a large opening on their snout. This made their skull less heavy.

Most reptiles' teeth are in shallow grooves. Archosaurs teeth were in sockets.

Where Did Triassic Dinosaurs Live?

Most of Earth's land was connected during the Triassic Period. This big area of land was called Pangea.

Pangea

Tethys
Sea

Panthalassic
Ocean

Pangea began to break apart in the late Triassic Period. The new pieces of land were called Laurasia and Gondwana.

Dinosaurs lived all over Earth in the late Triassic Period. Staurikosaurus (*store-rick-oh-sore-us*), liliensternus (*lil-ee-en-stur-nus*), and zupaysaurus (*zoo-pay-sore-us*) lived in different areas.

Liliensternus

Laurasia

Tethys Sea

Panthalassic Ocean

Gondwana

Staurikosaurus

Zupaysaurus

0 2,000 miles

0 4,000 kilometers (km)

N

Legend
☐ Land
☐ Ocean

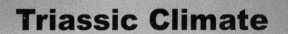

Triassic Climate

The Triassic Period had very hot, dry summers and cold winters.

There was a lot of rain in areas near the ocean.

Triassic Plants

Most of Pangea was a desert. There were not as many plants as there are today.

Many of the plants were ferns and trees with needles and pine cones.

Triassic Ocean Life

Most ocean animals in the Triassic Period were reptiles. Reptiles are cold-blooded animals who use the heat from the Sun to stay warm.

Nothosaurus (*noth-oh-sore-us*) was found in southwestern and eastern Asia, North Africa, and especially Europe.

One of the most common reptiles was ichthyosaur (*ik-thee-uh-sore*). They looked similar to today's dolphins.

Triassic Flying Creatures

Pterosaurs (*teh-ruh-sores*) were the first flying reptiles. Their wings were made from a thin skin called a membrane. This was similar to a bat's wings.

One of the first pterosaurs was eudimorphodon (*you-die-more-fo-don*). It had 110 teeth.

Kinds of Triassic Dinosaurs

One of the earliest known dinosaurs is called coelophysis (*seel-oh-fie-sis*). Coelophysis had a narrow head and lots of sharp teeth.

Herrerasaurus (*herr-ray-rah-sore-us*) had powerful back legs. This helped them run really fast.

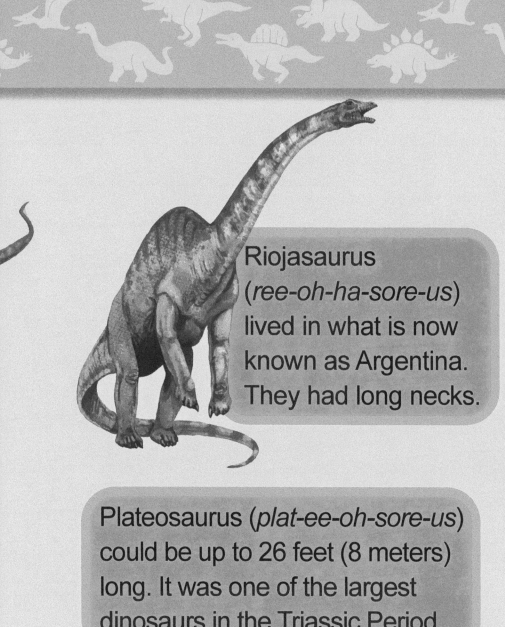

Riojasaurus (*ree-oh-ha-sore-us*) lived in what is now known as Argentina. They had long necks.

Plateosaurus (*plat-ee-oh-sore-us*) could be up to 26 feet (8 meters) long. It was one of the largest dinosaurs in the Triassic Period.

Curious Facts About the Triassic Period

The Triassic Period was named in 1834 after the three unique rock layers called the "Trias" found in Northern Europe.

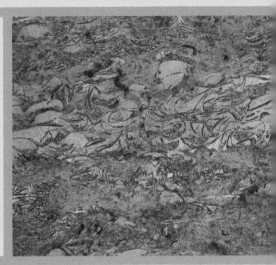

Almost all life on Earth was wiped out before the Triassic Period. This happened when Earth went through a very cold period.

There were no polar ice caps during the Triassic Period.

Mammals first appeared in the Triassic Period. Mammals are animals with warm blood and fur.

The temperature across most of Pangea was more than 100 degrees Fahrenheit (38 degrees Celcius).

The only new group of insects to appear during the Triassic Period were grasshoppers.

How Has the Triassic Period Impacted the World Today?

The first mammals appeared at the end of the Triassic Period. They mostly ate leaves or insects. The largest mammals were about the size of rats.

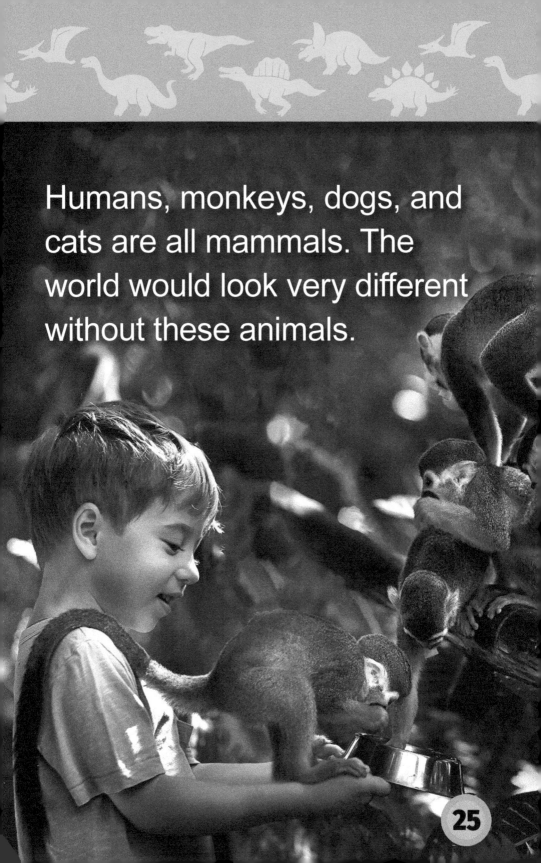

Humans, monkeys, dogs, and cats are all mammals. The world would look very different without these animals.

What Modern Animals Came From the Triassic Period?

An ancestor is someone related to you who lived a long time ago.

The ancestors of lizards, turtles, and crocodiles all first appeared in the Triassic Period.

How Did the Triassic Period End?

Many plants and animals went extinct at the end of the Triassic Period. This means they disappeared forever.

Some scientists think this happened because of volcanic eruptions. Others think that rapid changes in Earth's temperature ended the Triassic Period.

Quiz

Test your knowledge of the Triassic Period by answering the following questions. The questions are based on what you have read in this book. The answers are listed on the bottom of the next page.

1 When did the Triassic Period start?

2 What are dinosaurs from the Triassic Period called?

3 What was the big area of land in the Triassic Period called?

4 What were the first flying reptiles called?

5 What is the only new group of insects to appear during the Triassic Period?

6 When did mammals first appear?

Explore Our Engage Books Readers!

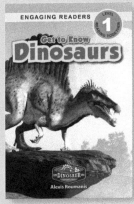

ENGAGING READERS · LEVEL 1 · READING TOGETHER

Get to Know Dinosaurs

Alexis Roumanis

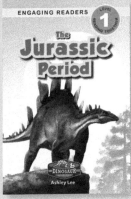

ENGAGING READERS · LEVEL 1 · READING TOGETHER

The Jurassic Period

Ashley Lee

ENGAGING READERS · LEVEL 1 · READING TOGETHER

The Cretaceous Period

Ashley Lee

ENGAGING READERS · LEVEL 1 · READING TOGETHER

The Solar System

Ashley Lee

ENGAGING READERS · LEVEL 1 · READING TOGETHER

Ladybugs

ANIMALS

Ashley Lee

ENGAGING READERS · LEVEL 1 · READING TOGETHER

Sharks

ANIMALS

Ashley Lee

ENGAGING READERS · LEVEL 2 · READING WITH HELP

Energy

Ashley Lee

ENGAGING READERS · LEVEL 2 · READING WITH HELP

Dogs

ANIMALS

Ashley Lee

ENGAGING READERS · LEVEL 2 · READING WITH HELP

Frogs

ANIMALS

Ashley Lee

Visit www.engagebooks.com to explore more Engaging Readers.

Answers:
1. About 252 million years ago 2. Archosaurs 3. Pangea 4. Pterosaurs 5. Grasshoppers 6. In the late Triassic Period